Portal of Dreams

Poems

Andrés Rodríguez

Poet Andrés Rodríguez's wonderful new book is a "sorcery of falling." With imagery both fierce and exquisite, these poems take the reader on a plummeting and soaring journey through the lives of the fallen and the trampled, and the ardent struggle to veer upward again into flight.

--Charlotte Zoë Walker, author of *Condor and Hummingbird, My Irish Grandmothers*, and editor of *The Art of Seeing Things*

Portal of Dreams crackles with life, mourns death, and senses the essence of human connections. In his finely shaped poems, Andrés Rodríguez travels from the city and its "crust of shattered nights" through desert revelations and on into deep history's "crowded tomb" and cruelties. He channels lost and wounded voices and communes with demons and dreams. This is just what you want in a book of poems: surprise and revelation on every page.

-- Steve Paul, author of *Hemingway at Eighteen* and editor of *Kansas City Noir*

Also by Andrés Rodríguez

Night Song

Book of the Heart: The Poetics, Letters, and Life of John Keats

We are such stuff as dreams are made on.

—William Shakespeare

PORTAL OF DREAMS

Poems by
Andrés Rodríguez

Woodley Press

2018

Published by Woodley Press, Washburn University, Topeka, KS

Cover art: Andros I. García Saldívar, *Plegarias, 2016*

Library of Congress Cataloging-in-Publication data

woodleypress.org

Acknowledgements

My gratitude to the editors of the following publications in which these poems first appeared:

The Alembic: "Self-Portrait"
The Americas Review: "The Leopard" and "Sueño" (formerly "The Death of Ernesto Trejo")
Bilingual Review: "El Abrazo" (formerly "For an Old Teacher"), "Chronicle of a Salvadoran Girl," and "Escondido"
Blue Mesa Review: "After the Discovery"
The Cortland Review: "Cicadas"
Diálogo: "Papa Cayo Meets a Demon on the Road to Mictlan"
Flashquake: "Postcard"
Flint Hills Review: "Looking Up and After," "The Nets by Caspar David Friedrich," and "Touch"
Harvard Review: "Central Street"
Hogtown Creek Review: "Strange Flight"
Houston Literary Review: "Portal of a Dream"
I-70 Review: "Desert Falls" and "An Open Letter to John Keats in Æternum"
Journal of Family Life: "Velorio"
Kansas City Hispanic News: "Malinche on Cortés"
Kansas City Star: "Milton's Taproom" and "Nacimiento"
New York Quarterly: "Everything is Dark"
Palabra: "Knives" (formerly "El Angelón") and "Memorial to the Fallen One"
Prairie Poetry: "The Harp"
River City Poetry: "New Home"
Yellow Medicine Review: "The Old Yaqui"

"Banners" appeared in *Currents from the Dancing River: Contemporary Latino Fiction, Nonfiction, and Poetry*, edited by Ray González, Harcourt.

My thanks to David W. Foster, whose friendship and mentoring have been life sustaining. And to W. S. Di Piero, without whose example there would be no invention and witness.

Contents

En el recuerdo de mi padre

1

Central Street

Awake to gunshots
loud fuzzy music
overdubbing
the wail of sirens
blues and reds
of squad cars
lashing my room
everywhere out there
stars fade
in here dreams sink
to dark pools
I rise once more
walk out the door
to see a crust
of shattered nights
sneakers on powerlines
a skyward leap
arrested
and a black light
combing the street
from all the eyes
that spread it.

Cicadas

Louder now, they weave their song
among the trees, grappled onto branches
where wind never upends them,
where summer strikes fire into a voice.
Like old pipers wheezing the same
crazed note between catches of breath,
they sit in their unreachable height
and drone that underground music
after seven or seventeen years,
raucous lords of the air and earth.

How do they sleep so long in darkness
beneath the surface noise of the earth?
How do they know it's time to rise up
in the hottest month of the year?
What do they see after those murky years
with tiny eyes like beads of blood?
It must be memory's old bright place,
the first desert, prairie, swamp, or wood,
where their cries came bubbling up
to terrify or tire creation's other forms.

A man on my block who worked nights
once shotgunned the trees outside his house
as if that would stop the buggy music.
But as the smoke cleared, it arose at once,
and that man fell back silent, nameless,
drained by those agonizers of throatless song.
When I lie sleepless in my room, unable
to dream or breathe the pressured air,
the sound in my ears pierces my heart
with dusty white pincers, unkillable.

As a boy I'd see one fall from the sky,
wrapped with a hornet in a death-embrace.
They'd land in a blur on sidewalk or grass
and a prolonged shriek let loose—
not like any laugh or cry I'd ever heard,
but still a screeching or beseeching
that arced the air with a zinc flash
whose cinders fell on everything.
I'd watch the brief struggle until
death arose with a king in his arms.

The sudden chill felt back then
comes now with a buzz heard in
chicharras, whose slangy meaning
is electric cattle prods. Somewhere
a torturer enters a cell or brightly lit room
with one of these ravagers of burning steel.
Its blackened head sparks and crackles,
searing the genitals of a woman or man
whose suffering feeds the lords of death,
whose terror lasts a thousand thousand years.

Milton's Taproom

Tonight my ghosts quiver back:
neon-blued barstools, sweating tumblers,
briny gold mirrored bottles in their slots,
and music's cool dark lofting vibe.
They charm the space of the parking lot
where I once reverberated in the night.

Progress defeated me before the last call
for beers and shots, before the last set
of drums and sax. My doors closed,
my rooms grew cold, and the squads
of insipid city bureaucrats razed all.
The lovers at my tables will never shine again.

But my true body lies in sound,
ecstatic iteration, not brick or glass.
Inside the megastore, where the midtown
shoppers have gone home, I bare my heart
in red fluorescence and pour out
Basie, Ellington, and Bird's lost blues.

I wind my song around the city.
Two million circulating lives.
A train yearning for the sea.
And then an icy Christmas scene unfolds,
jazzmen swaying in a tight corner,
red and green bulbs canopied overhead.

The crowd edges the stage, gathered
like herdsmen abiding in the dark.
The live song is a passage to the stars,
a voyage to the far side of the rim,
where snow falls, the sea overflows,
and we all hear another song before it begins.

Escondido

He keeps to his room,
dancing inside the beat—
salsa, mambos, boleros,
songs that can't carry him
back to what he lost
in a cinder-gray sky.
La tierra bonita.

He got in trouble fast,
the new kid in a gang
of other people's sons.
Latin Kings or Malditos,
it's all the same:
the brotherhood of
fucked-up nerves.

He pissed someone off.
A fight over a girl,
or a word that wouldn't
stay in his mouth:
puto, joto, maricón.
It makes no difference.
He's the one without a gang,
Abel beaten but not killed,
menaced by his brother
who stalks the walls of night,
who hides wherever he is.

Many nights they hunted him,
fired shots into his home.

Then the stolen cars set ablaze
and crashed into his porch.
This went on for months.

He never leaves his room,
thinking dust his only place,
the walls made for that.
Through his window
the flow of night brings
headlights, a squeal of tires,
some word that won't stay.

Little by little he is
disappearing into the music
that throbs across the air
of alien Kansas City.
Soon he'll be a scarf of breath
tangled on powerlines
that cross the heavens like nets
and let nothing slip through.

Self-Portrait

Still unused ornaments of dust,
    flaked gold leaf among fluted stem glass
in tiny piles of hush, clothes
    and clogs flung in a corner,
        as if lives had departed there—
all these and more you once
    sought to bring you joy,
        joy that sags before me
in your third-floor walk-up,
    in perfect isolation.

I see the grief in things. I see you,
    my first love, staring back at me
from the glow of the bathroom door,
    whose dingy light reaches into
        the recesses of your disarray.
Then a small voice asks,
    "Who are you? What do you want?"
        I turn toward the sound,
    and what catches my eye is a painting,
        frameless, on the floor.

Here is an imaginary street
    with a BAR sign over the sidewalk,
on a night dark as a jeweler's cloth.
    You've placed yourself in the center
        from where you come forward,
a sixteen-year-old beauty in a red dress.
    The wind slips between your legs
        and lifts the hem as you smile.

The longer I stare, the greater the beauty
        gleaming against that black cloth of night.

But there is more. On a bench sits a man,
    elbows on knees, face in hands,
agony frozen by the sinew of weeping.
    On the street behind you,
        a one-legged man on crutches
leans into the wind that flays his clothes.
    In the center of all, you seem
            removed, untouched,
        or tingling with some knowledge
            that plays upon the scene.

Sobs from the television downstairs.
    Or somebody's dreamtime begun.
You stare at me still, lost in the light,
    and I remember wanting love
            to spring from the pages of books
        and make the starry lights of this city
lift off ground, bound for other worlds,
            lifting me out of this life as well.

What happened to that girl I knew?
    Did you leave her behind
to gather the nightworld around her,
    queen of the skid row subjects?
        Or did she refuse the living stream
        to wander the night, leaving you
stranded in cluttered rooms
        repeating that question of who and what?

Here in your self-portrait, her smile says
        nothing I recognize at all,
even if I could compose the missing stories
        of you. She steps over the sidewalk,
                moving against harsh or weepy air,
        always coming forward in time,
always drawing nearer,
                never arriving.

Velorio

Old relations return
(This is your *madrina*)
and lost ones stand apart
(Oh, him? A second
cousin to somebody).
At McGilley's Midtown,
we sit talking on a sofa
below a frescoed blue sky
while the chapel fills up—
perfume, aftershave,
roses, sweat, and cigarettes
sickening my senses.
I remember the plush red
carpet catching my shoes
when I was led to a box
holding a form so unlike
my flesh. Its face was cork,
a shadow on a snow-bed,
a mummy without scarab,
an absent uncle sleeping
amid shudders and tears.
Here now it's my mother,
who still looks pained,
who lies as if on stones,
whose flesh unbecomes my own.

I scarcely remember her,
only the living ghost
sitting beside other shades
abandoned to machines—

revolving wheels of blood,
leached out memory.
And for seven dark years,
sundered from his bride,
my father slept alone,
enduring her nights with Death.
Yet through the darkness
some small bubble arose
that shone dimly inside
hospital, car, and house,
some prismatic globe
that treasured them
as they looked out at me
standing watch.   "Blessed
art thou among women,"
intones the priest, and the call
in separate voices that make
one long ascending cry
twists my heart here below.
The words that come to me
are soft, small, like apology:
"I have no child, I have
nothing but a book,
nothing but that to prove
your blood and mine."

When it's finally over—
the handshakes, the hugs,
the kisses searing my cheek—
I watch my father hobble
casket side and reach in
to touch uncanny coldness.

He waits, silted flesh,
and in that pause I hear
their low secret voices
(unweeping, firm in love)
with nothing to say to us
as they flee the parlor sky.

Sueño

We're all here, packed in the family car,
she-of-my-dreams behind the wheel, squinting.

She can't drive worth shit;
she plows into trees, cars, still squinting.

"Don't look at me!" she screams,
"If you look at me I'll have to keep squinting!"

Her face sours on the space between two cars
like tiny letters she can read only by squinting.

I put my hand on her shoulder;
she vapors into a dream, hearing the night

of words I whisper in her ear
that repeat the strings of night.

We watch her alone in the woods
practicing archery bathed in silvery night,

her face bright as the river's icy run.
"This arrow is for you,

and this for you, for you, for you . . ."
the moon pale and mute falling through the night.

Knives

The morning before he died,
my father decided to
sharpen the kitchen knives.
He was silent, ashen,
weaker day by day,
but he smoothly worked each blade
like a skater on a slaty lake
and filled the house
with the sound of preparing.

Later I asked him
to take a spin with me
in the old Ford.
He sat waiting,
watching cars and buses
storm past our view,
the windows of a distant high-rise
black as the peepholes of a tower.
He watched
and waited in silence.

That night I could hear him
in the room next to mine,
loud deep breaths indrawn,
followed by rackety gusts.
I was used to his weather,
like a bird sleeping in the wind,
and I dropped off
to his 200-pound snore
pooling into dreams.

Then at 3 a.m.
the wingbeats,
the growling,
the rough dialogue.
I heard my father
draw the knives,
enraged and hateful
toward the dark.
I heard him slash
and grunt, giving
or taking a blow.

But what good against
the swift arrival,
the strength of the wings,
the power of the sword?
What chance when
eternal night
bursts into the room,
snow swirling in the air,
and a hulking shadow
breathless there?

At dawn I entered
the darkened space where
silence flowed out and in.
He was there on his bed,
the sheets balled at his big feet.
He was there on his side,
so very still, heavier.
He was there, alone,
in his finished time,
the knives a pale shimmer on the floor.

The Leopard

Many nights as stars swirl in darkness
I have a recurrent dream of a leopard.
Last night it was sitting outside my door
head still, erect, gold eyes in the gloom
holding me in their radiance, freezing me
with their sleepy fury. Then its loins
began to pulse under shadowy spots
that floated like ashes loosed from fire.
The jaws crossed the air and clamped
my hands, my vexed, whitened hands.
I knew I was in the cave of sleep,
in the night's long fitful hush, but I
could only watch the leopard, there,
make me its own with the starry points of its eyes.

2

Kore

You have nothing to do with gardens,
what breaks forth at harvest.
Not oozing honey, grain, or leaves,
light and air disclosing spring.
And if your hand trembles,
it's not with fear but anticipation
to taste the bloody orb and burst
those seeds of hell upon your tongue.

Anemone, iris, primrose, poppy
fall through a cleft in earth
to black bottoms of tears.
You weren't dragged down,
you leapt, speeding after love,
swelling like a fruit with the gift
the shadows bloomed when you felt
the rough impress of a father's sunless kiss.

Touch

"I can't get my mind around it," she says,
cold quicksilver beading in the IV,
heavy urine bag dark below the bed.
The wall clock clumps out loud.
She stares at nothing, then resumes talk
of family, school, jobs won and lost,
all but the mind's big trouble.
Consciousness hangs over the brink,
numbed by drugs that don't work.
Only the revolving door of doctors and nurses
wakes her to the retchy smell of herself.
She stops in midsentence.
Nervous I ask, "How's Mia been?"
Suddenly her eyes lock mine
and she reaches out her hand—
long bony fingers levitating above
the sheer blanket that drapes her
thin bloated body, pallid underneath.
I take it, surprised by the warmth
that knocks inside her fingertips,
though the grip is light and weak,
the bones sharp as knives.

    I'm almost afraid this moment.
Then while waiting for words
that don't come, I remember
Tara and her husband, Mia and me,
we four in a circle, smoking pot,
laughing, laughing hard, in tears,
feeling like caged animals now
released and removed from time.

I gazed at their faces lit up
by the single candle between us,
my pupils spread and receiving
its gold that reached everywhere.
The music on the stereo looped in the room,
the singer's words such intense arousal.
She grabbed my knee and leaned into
the halo of my senses, laughter still
breaking from her body in waves
that spun me inside each swirl
like a bee drunk with sweet blooms.
I thought she spoke to no one but me,
though I heard only laughter's music.
    For months after that night,
I craved some sign or word ("Come").
I followed her around on double-dates
scented with her loose hair.
I pictured her fleshy thighs to myself
and the padded valley they led to.
I waited for her laugh to spin me
again with its warm sliding waves.
When she smiled, another life
opened for me to enter, without
the lure and rebuff her sister plied.
Mia was the angel of remoteness,
guardian of her virginal innocence,
closed as a flower at night.
She appeased me with merest touch—
hand on arm, pale neck, heart—
and though I hoped for more, I was
stretched between *hold close* and *let go*
until that moment's vagrant touch
filled me with a new half-defined hope.

Yet it fled or faded
like an echo into a darkness
deeper and blacker than night,
where the open hand waits.
Tara left her husband, Mia and I
broke up, each of us vanishing,
the circle abandoned, the animals
snared. And after all these years,
called into a stark white room,
called now to wait upon an edge,
I ask myself why I came here.
Not for old times. Not for love.
Maybe for the stilled longing
overflowing this room. I face her
whose touch I burned for once,
whose fear I can't now soothe.

Raised up on a last cold bed,
her hand still in mine, she presses
firmly, draws me in close to her
wasted face, wets blanched
crusted lips with tongue tip, breath
sucked of all that once was sweet.
I feel dizzy from attraction to her—
or is it death itself? In the silence,
released from craving or thought,
I enter a place where hands twine
more fluent than laughter's ghosts,
where touch, because answered,
deepens, not upsets, the mind,
and calls out a joy memory can trust.
"Do you remember?" I begin.
She stares a while till at last "Sorry"
spills from her lips. "There's nothing

to be sorry about," I assure,
and her smile leaves a blessing on the air.
I tell her I must go so she can rest.
Her hand drops away, the clock
resumes its march, and the IV now
is an hourglass drained of sand.
I step to the door, about to enter
the outer noisy flow. "Come
see me again," she says.
I turn and say, "I will."

Under Eiffel

From the clouds I saw the Emerald Isle,
solid and lush below me, and imagined
its pastures, orisons, thorny flames.
Landing in Amsterdam, I took a train
that evening which ran toward Paris,
where a galaxy of streets, black with
March rain, taught me likeness
burdened with darkening desire.
I saw a woman pass light and silent
under a streetlamp, trailing rainlight
that spindrifted up the heavy air.
She looked too much like you
who passed here long before me,
leaving what night and desire retrieve—
this black rain and buried streets of the heart.

Téléphone

Île de la Cité

Its buttons are full moons,
a calendar year of them,
wolfing down your coins
into its dark dry den.

How many faint spoogings
of desire has it heard?
How many secrets locked
in spotless bowels?

Your blood knows the numbers,
though they've disappeared
in this metaxy of streetlights
and melting corpulent fog.

Your call canals farmlands,
outstrips nightwings, doubles
back at the sight of flames,
then bursts through tunnels,

lasers across the Atlantic,
until emerging on circuitry
with the new world's love's grief
trembling as names and signs.

Listen. You'll hear clicks,
metallic murmurs, jails unbolting,
then the easy heat of a voice.
Allô amour! Qu'est-ce que tu portes?

Everything Is Dark

Everything totters here in Nogales.
Cardboard shanties spill down the hills
like dinghies listing in a frozen wave.
In the avenue traffic, a peddler hawks
cheap gold watches on both arms
up to elbows. Cars brake,
tires squeal, and our ears can't mute
the blaring music of the district,
a Mexicoland where you never get lost.

We go like spies among the tourists,
browsing the vendors whose smiles
flay us because we don't buy.
Then I see the *traje* inside a doorway.
She nurses a baby and watches the street.
A toddler beside her pats the tiled floor
with both hands. As we approach,
she stretches out an open palm:
¡Para los niños! ¡Para los niños!

I'm ripped from this moment,
pitched toward another, underground,
where her twin, in a faded *sari*,
sitting on the Paris subway floor,
cries in French for the infant
whose reedy head sags at her breast.
An outstretched skinny fist balls her words.
I feel the greasy whoosh of subway cars
before I hear the screech of tracks

echoing off tiled walls farther below.
The longer I stare, the more her words
bleed into footsteps, car horns, Mariachi rant—
a storm of sounds falling world to world.
Then I see that shadowed face and empty
hand fluttering like a flower between us.
The air grows dark. Under my feet
the pavement is mold black. I walk away.
The beggars, hucksters, and shanty sleepers

send up a cry that balls its fist tighter every day.
I look back, feeling her words.
The hand withdraws from sun to shade,
a tiny drop into broken city sounds
that box her in there looking out
through quiet bitter eyes. I lose her
in the setting light that floods brick, glass,
steel shutters, and the few straggly trees,
then closes round us like a mouth.

Strange Flight

Look at them fall! Look up at the sky!
Black angels groaning to earth!
Wheels grinding on waves of air!
They fall, all, three figures now
sheeted air, chasing one another
to a music that spells and speaks me,
a churning whirlpool-eye,
spiraling down to the mark.

When they land on desert floor,
pulling torn wings and tails
inside themselves, I know he has
mine, she, his, and I everyone's,
as three become one shadow moving—
a sky-born creature that will never die
until it hatches pain out of earth.

Devils Tower

Night had not yet come
when we saw it growing bigger
and closer until it stood
like nothing under sky.
No tree or castle ever gave such a jolt.
Magma darkened.
Earth ooze blackened.
I thought of pyramids, sacrifice,
arterial blood rivering down the air.
What you thought I never knew—
you always watched silent,
without a voice to spare.

Tourists. Parking lot. Rangers.
We moved against the flow,
anonymous mute pair
in the presence of a titan,
a moon chunk on earth,
a star-gazer's island shrine
indifferent to worship.
I could feel you wrap
the blackness around you,
imagination's palette,
just as you could hear my words
shaping and mingling dreams.

Side by side we circled,
spiraled, veered, dissolved,
while that stone in the center,
static as the sun, a dead sun,
shone above and below the earth.
It was like water reflecting sky,
or sky reflecting water,
I can't explain it after all these years
making, unmaking, remaking,
I see where our life reversed,
but I don't know how,
I don't know why.

We never came back from
that moment, that motion,
though the journey ended.
Only in dreams have I returned,
you beside me no longer silent,
telling me how stone is a gift
and dark hills are so beautiful.

Desert Falls

By March the sun rose quicker than it should,
sending us to the mountains for relief
from swaths of hell that convulsed the valley.
You were in your element among the rocks,
cactus, and gem-hoards of the sands,
three steps ahead of me, taking those
barren steeps overlooking our desert city
which glinted like broken glass in a junk lot.

I had followed you to the razored border,
cutting myself from home for you.
Each day felt like a year in an oven,
each night an eternity under tons of stars.
I couldn't cross this vast open space,
this empire of noon. From a window,
I watched wind's dry white breath
while sitting in sweat-ruined clothes.

As we neared the secret falls
that spilled a pool we never found,
I was hoping to get beyond
the wrath of thorns, the unsparing
waves of light, and enter where they end—
bluish caves with depths outspread,
the last high springs where tiny fish
in membranous time faintly glow.

When we paused on the gravelly trail
to take in the cliffs and a caracara above,
I tumbled down the bajada as if pushed

by ghostly hands that wouldn't let me pass,
the rocks like grinding breakers
rolling me to a sea I drank and drank.
As I fell—your face turning toward
or from me, I couldn't tell which—

the wavering sky doubled into a watery
brightness. I slid into the underbrush
that closed around me with a click.
I wanted to call, to cry your name,
but couldn't stop this sorcery of falling,
this rush toward sand where I felt
pinned against a solar furnace and
heard every creature pause in midsong.

Portal of a Dream

At dawn I see a shadow
crossing your face below
the blue repose of skin.
It is edgeless
like hummingbird wings
thrumming before they
zip through space.
Awoken by this flight
or my stare, your mouth
flutters open, eyes still
closed, and then words
crack through to tell me
where you've been.

"I was by the sea.
A woman there had
three babies sleeping
inside her. I saw them
through her skin!
They clung tenderly
to each other, so
tenderly, each face
a future asleep.
I helped the woman
get in a rowboat
to sail the waves alone.
As I watched from shore,
a storm was growing
and everything got still
before it went dark."

You fall silent now,
gazing at what was.
Deep in the quiet
we hold together,
entangled again,
I dream my way into
your voice to find
one afternoon's
sun-drenched floor
we danced across,
bare feet leaving pools
that fled once seen.
It hurt to face such
ordinary brightness,
such casual daytime
splendor, because I see
the end in all things
no matter how hard
I try to seine
beauty's brief sight.
And here I am again
trying to live into what I see.

Slim delicate toes.
Thick bony heels.
We danced till we saw
our faces peering back
from the wall mirror.
You said our children
would be a mixed circuitry
of water and earth.
Then we saw a face,

bred by the late day's
shifting hues, gaze back
from that portal of glass,
luminous as the sea.

Though safe in the
mooring of arms,
I feel low thunder,
wings in every corner,
shadows to come
while we sleep.
I resist myself—
the absence feared
and learned by love.
I want to wake
and see you bright
as sunlight, sharing
the room and dawn.
I don't have to dream
to know how your face
reflects the light of water.
Maybe one day I'll see
the woman of life,
changeless and changing,
and call to her across
the ocean's vast dream.

Under the Mountain

On your sixtieth birthday, I'll be daisies.
But oh, to be Forget-me-nots
planted by you long past!
Yet even before then
time will have likely erased
every trace of me in you,
like crematory fire vaporizing
the last drops of the heart.
Against such light, such power,
memory's a coin under the mountain.
But I won't care then,
I'll be ruled by the underlords,
coined by darkness,
my only light from the house of Tláloc,
faint as the white of your breasts
once pillowed in my sleep.
By the glow of all your birthday cakes,
by the evening light filling your dress,
try to remember then
the mind and body of love
that opened before you.
When I'm just a penny in the ocean,
call my name to light up the night and conjure
the amber of your arms,
the honey of your breath,
the beauty that once quickened life.

3

After the Discovery

Jamaica. 29th February 1494.

Nothing shamed him. Not the lies he told
with his superb indifference to the truth,
not even the killings by his men
when they wanted food. Deliberate, blank,
he looked upon his island kingdom
as he looked upon the natives' faces—
something to justify, pure and simple.
He'd lost his boyish dreams the last voyage
and became a man of willed destiny.
This time when the admiral sighted land,
he jumped down to the sandy white beach
and on his haunches said to the tree line:
"Bless you all, children, I'm an original.
I have worse in store for you than fear."
He had all that jungle to enter, all that
alien flesh switching through the leaves.
But what did he do this time?
More hawk bells and glass beads
to bargain his way to Cipangu.
He did not know this was a new world;
he believed he was still in the old.
"I deem it wise we hasten," he pronounced.
But where to? There was no Cipangu.

One day his ire rose hot as the sun,
for the Indians wanted their brethren—
his captive women and children—ransomed.
He bade his scholars to disclose their lore,
and they spoke of a lunar eclipse that night,

one that would plunge the hemisphere
for an hour in utter darkness. I felt
the hilarious intent inside his head.
He came out of his closet and stood alone,
firelight dancing like ghosts on his face,
and said his God would bloody the moon
if they did not help God's messengers.
The look of disbelieving children
as the first stars pierced the purple sky.
And he felt glad, returning to his closet.
Soon the moon wore a puckered brown face,
and the ground, once white as snow,
darkened as if there was no moon at all.
From his closet he felt the noise in the air
and waited for the moment to reemerge,
saying his God had restored the moon.
He could have been paring his nails or
poking the last embers with his sword.

Soon the Indians were sent to the mines.
I have seen them return from underground,
shackled to one another, hands and feet
profusely bleeding, Christlike heads
pulled down to limping shadows.
I have followed them into the mine's
foul stench, down the long chute,
their rattling chains strung out the length
of humid walls, a dismal song inside.
Descending, I have expected a prospect
of silver and gold, fruits of the earth,
the crown's wealth spread at my boots,
but instead seen bones light up the dark,
a cold resurrection in this crowded tomb.

Malinche on Cortés

*The Amerindian guide and translator
for Hernan Cortés speaks.*

I was happy to be his,
that goat with the black beard,
for he listened with respect
and heeded my counsel
when I became his tongue.
With him I owned my desires.
Long ago my own people
gave me away to strangers
to glut a stepfather's wrath.
I forgave them, even Mother,
who was wife before mother,
who trembled at my return
beside the prophesied lord
with glory and spoils of war.
Calling me his queen,
he gave me jade beads
to give away. Yet I knew
he wanted gold, not jade,
which irritated him.
He would help or hurt
to meet his need, always
driven like a harlot for more.
When we entered the capitol,
I, too, was dazzled by
the soaring temples
and quetzal feathers
and carved jade masks.
See this ring?
From Tenochtitlán.

When the end came
(it's easy to remember)
he sat on a mound of skulls,
a new kind of priest,
listening to the city murmur
in the fires his men set.
That clarity of mind,
that instinct for success
was like terror's holiness
in Tiger, Snake, or Hawk.
What he was like at night
is the punishment in fullness
that still sings in my veins.
O Martín! Son!
I wanted you always inside me.
He belongs to the Tyrant
who left me in this cell
beyond the doomed city
while he sailed home across
the waters of Anáhuac.
The world belongs to his kind—
soldiers, users, inventors of new words,
who drive the nail home
when there's nothing more to win.
Now I circle myself in myself
as the air sobs "love."
Is it my thought
or his mockery
taking over my thought?
O Mexicans! O children!
Malinche tells you
our lives move together like a wave.

The Old Yaqui

When I was young I learned to read and write
from the Spanish priest who said Mass each day
in the mission church. It took him years
to teach me the swarming hived words in his breviary
because I played dumb all the while eating
those snaky sounds—*deus, pax vobiscum, spiritu.*
I was hungry for a world I could not name.
I tried to send my spirit into the words,
wrestle them, make them obey me.
In my dreams I stood on a hill beholding
the Holy Ghost enter a hawk that tumbled
down clouds and canyons, bird of my core.
He told me, *Bear it away, what is given.*
Alone in hushed sacristy's strawberry light
I studied till the words flew off my tongue
and up the air, black wings looking for a kill.
At night I wrote lines in the filth on my own skin.
My brothers watched afraid and tried to keep me in my place.
When I killed the priest, I ran to the hills crowing,
Bear it away! I will bear it all away!

Papa Cayo Meets a Demon on the Road to Mictlan

The demon appears in the form of a large dog and speaks.

Saludos, Cayo, it's me again,
dripping wormy wetness
from the earth. Risen!
No, don't run away, amigo.
I want to talk, pues,
here in the moonlight.
Years I've watched you
from between cracks
and through glassy lakes,
your thin shoesoles
like two tongues of dust.
You're a pious fellow
with a shifty streak,
just like your father,
and his, back to Adán.
After all these years
I can still find you
swapping trinkets
con indios y pelados
in the wilds of Zocapu.
N'ombre, put away
your pistola. Behold
this light within my eye.
You can cross yourself
but can't drive me away
like a ghost haunting
dead husks of corn.
Go on, call your saints,
eat your words and letters.

My names have power, too:
Diablo. Chamuco. Pingo.
Satanás. Lucifero. Xolotl.
I spread fire with this eye.
My houses are next to
churches—when I yowl
it's hard for men to pray.
We demons choose when
to turn wishes to doubts,
madden the taste of desire,
then move in at twilight,
a hill of shadows,
to take you.
We're busy every day,
unlike Boss Juan who's
always eating pan dulce,
drinking pulque, absent
from the wretched land.
We break our necks just
to sow a little discontent.
And what an effort
to bore into dreams, giving
your waking hours fits!
It's all a dog can do
to tear out your throat.
Won't you tickle my chest
or scratch behind my ear?
I see you'd rather not
as I am smelly and hot
from all the filth and fire
through which I've trod,
dogging your heels.
I'd like to talk more,

but I must slip a stranger's
hand in a child's and spit
a little rain to cover it up.
You can go now, pues.
I'll leave you for a while,
but understand,
the way these things go,
I'll be back after
you leave your town
and head for gringo-land,
where bad luck will
dog your days, where
your children will disobey,
and your woman fall
into madness;
the gabacho will turn
from wrath to indifference
to wrath again,
and one day
you'll be thinking of
a life you could have lived,
and it'll be me again,
up from the earth,
looking right into your eyes.

Banners

El Monte, California, 1933

Our men never smoked
and drank only water,
safe under the walnut tree,
enfolded by great arms
upholding June sunlight.
They came each day as dawn
approached, tense somber men
crowding together and speaking
low in the presence of
the morning star. We women
could hear the winds shifting
south over empty fields.

Hours passed. Our children
chewed sticks like ears of corn,
dust-devils danced and died
in the road. The sheriffs passed
at noon in steaming black cars.
Nothing looked changed—
the same huddled shacks
below the sun, dungarees
sagging on clotheslines.
So they passed on, riding out
the horizon as our singers
plucked a noisy chord.

When they emerged, stiff,
morose, the evening rattle
started in the trees. *Tomorrow*

we march to the fields, they said.
We brought them a sip of coffee
cooled by the night wind and
watched their faces screw up
as they waved goodnight
and turned home over fields
brimming with fruit.

                    *

Soon the strikebreakers came.
And then the sheriffs lured our
men into the station with
lies, promises of good work.
And the Mexican consul there
sporting a pencil-stick moustache,
a solemn porky bastard who
sprouted among our dazed men
calling them "reds." After that
we kept up the daily pickets
and mass meetings and prayers.

The first time we drove trucks
through town, forty women,
shouting, making the place
a bee hive, raw sunburnt faces
stared at us on every street.
That was all right. But one man,
alone, swore at us. Bracing
his hips by the roadside,
hard blue eyes burning through us,
he wished us bloodied and raped.
I never knew why the town

existed, but now I knew that
seeing it, my own heart was
staring at itself, blood
running not singing.

Returning at twilight,
I watched the dark fields slipping
past, the air hot, always doubled,
smell of youngberries rotting.
Now I could no longer find hope,
because we buried three children
and put the sticks they chewed
upon that ground, one on each grave,
there in the summer harvest light.

                  *

I can still see those stars
poking through the roof slats,
green, blue, and plum red.
Eyes shut, I imagined rolling
on a wave of lights as if
the night sky were a sea.
I never dreamt of food.
That night I woke to a small
tapping on the roof, the room
cool, spread out like a wood.
My husband slept, his tangled
hair on my arm, mouthing words
that have always stayed with me:
Ya 'cabaron todo!

The hour comes back in the dust
thick with panicked men. Harsh cries
sang out from the workers throwing
their heads behind them, a sheet
of lightning across yellow clouds,
then the crack like a thunderstorm.
Three were blasted, rolling into
a ditch where they lay face down,
licking the mossy earth. Some
were pulled away screaming, *Brothers!*
Murderers! Then we scattered
like nightmare leaves over the valley.

Letter from Midtown

Taped to the window of a public storage building.

Looking for the girl
who stood in line with me
7-Eleven last April
Main & Armour.
We talked about snow
high as stop signs
and blowing this town
December in Orlando.
Sat together
in the parking lot.
Twinkies beer & smokes.
Remember?
Forgot your name
sounded like *hay-dee*.
I see with my ears
and they work slow.
Been gone six months
home in South Dakota
nothing but snow
rusted cars & no job.
The oil rigs, silos, Kmarts
all different now
ghosts on the headlands.
Only your laugh
coming on the air
500 miles away
day after day
runs thru me.
Left two weeks ago
burned my tracks.
Hoping to meet again.
Ready for ocean
a bed on the beach.

If you see this
look for me in
coin laundries
Mickey Ds
bus shelters
tunnels where I sleep
my car dead on I-29
tagged & towed by now.
I'm here and there
Jon Buffalo
a bit thinner.
Leave reply.

Chronicle of a Salvadoran Girl

When I met her
(and pardon me for saying so)
she was a peach.
Any man could gobble her up with just a look,
or strip her little by little
of dress and modesty
till she was naked, helpless.

Always that same smiling girl,
at ease and full of life—
but some were jealous of her charms,
others proud that one of their own
set so high an example.

When I met her,
she went to high school basketball games,
read the society news in the paper
and Red Pillow romance novels.
Well, yes, she dreamed.
She built her castles in the air
and had a blue prince who loved her.
(for her everything blue was love.)
She went to dances, wearing
tight sweaters and pants
pasted on her hot tits and ass,
yet secretly wished she'd drop her slipper
and jumped for joy to see a black Porsche slicing the air.

Her story is terrible.

When I met her,
she liked to hear the homeboys' come-ons,
the bold music of their whistles.
She went through the streets like a champ,
too great even to fit on the sidewalk.
The whole city watched her,
and no one knew she existed.
She crossed parks, porticoes, plazas, window-shopping.
She smiled, buying happiness wholesale.
She surpassed fortune, smiled again,
and turned homeward.
The neighbors loved her, hated her, sighed for her.
Again they placed her nude over the tender grass of desire.
It was finally something marvelous
having her at pointblank range.

Her story is terrible
and ordinary.

It was easy to know her
and wear her like a boutonniere,
and show her off to preppy girls,
to jocks who cheat on their exams,
to wankers in public johns,
hell, even to dirty old men with bad dye jobs,
all those filthy, lying codgers
who have no country, no leader, no god at all.

This girl's case is common.

When I met her, she never really cried,
except for a couple of tantrums crowned with tears,
and once when something got in her eyes.

What a girl after our own heart!
What loveliness!
What aimlessness!

Enough of that.

But what a Christian child!
What tender veal for sale!

I saw her. I felt for her.
I pushed her. I left her.
We have her.

There she is—
among desires without streets,
among obscene words,
among old geezers in cheap wigs,
among rendezvous in hip joints,
among jobs that yield no lovers,
among dried up, frustrated bosses,
among shadows growing colder, deeper in anguish,
among rumors that never speak a word of truth,
and looks that never speak at all . . .
From mouth to mouth, there is she.
We have her.

In all her disgrace, there she is.
Her and me, alone together,
without finding ourselves or each other.
We have no way out, but still I sing.
She cries or gives in. It's all the same.

(After José Roberto Cea's *Crónica de una muchacha salvadoreña*)

Memorial to the Fallen One

At last I've fallen like fiery tears.
They'll see my face in the mirror no more,
crying with all the dead below.
The blue tattered night leaves me
in empty space without statues or angels.

If you've any doubt,
I am that lump that closes your throat.

Someone says,
"Who'd believe in him?
He's fallen. And yet
he made even the stones speak."

Another adds,
"I've seen his traces,
and not a twilight remains.
He's disappeared like a new moon.
But someone will try to deny me
the right to enjoy his anguish—
anguish like an old orange bitten by the sun."

The fallen has fallen,
but he'll come again.
Raising himself,
he'll rise for the journey.

If I'm the fallen one,
it's because no one can raise me.
If I'm the fallen one,

it's so that the lost may rise and walk.

To enter silence
you must make silence.
That's why I've fallen—
so that someone hear its beginning.

To fall is not to hide or lose the way,
nor die for no reason.
To fall is to expect the other face,
the blood restored, the blank farewell,
the treasure blooming like the dawn.

I began by falling at my arrival.
The fear came later, but I risked the pain.
No one appeared as memory dissolved,
failing in the middle of remembering.
You've begun a new circle now.
You've gained innocence fully.

(After José Roberto Cea's *Memorial del caído*)

4

The Harp

Here on the prairie,
      no wind
            writes the world.
The unheard
      silver music
            breaks evening's
quieter surface,
      finishing the light,
            the hour.
Now dragonflies,
      etheric blue flames,
            black eyes lidless,
dance in the heart's ear,
      a dance I can't sing
            but have here
amid countless fires
      braiding
            memory in smoke.
How I love the strum
      and tone of it
            fallen from
the bowl,
      the womb above
            the graves.

for Denise Levertov (1923-1997)

Postcard

This is just to let you know
I got your card today,
the one with the ancient town
nestled below blue hills,
a deep drop in the foreground,
men and dogs hunting deer.

You never gripe about cancer—
too Midwestern, too stiff-spined
for overt whining. But I know
you smolder even in your dreams
how they cooked your breasts,
though you got to keep one.

I know too you'd never bare them
now, shielding like a virgin with
fluttering hands, your look searching
through me for the body you remember
as your heart ticks toward some
unknown explosion you're owed.

That middle age of custom—
small towns, woods, sporting life,
lovers drawing curtains, a bell calling
or warning through the streets—
has come to an end like a story.
Still ahead is another tale.

El Abrazo

A gnawed stick. That's what he looked like
when I saw him last. His long body
swayed against a steady son at his arm.
He was not the man who once stood flowering
at the lectern; not the man whose voice
rose and swept over the room, opening
that place apart from me in which he lived,
a place among words on the page.

No, it was another man who submitted to agony.
But still those sunken eyes shone in ecstasy,
seeing one more thing among many treasures
to learn from, to feast the mind on, the world
and its pain, that it would disappear in him, with him.
Or maybe he was walking clear of this last hurt,
his body leading into radiance step by wobbly step,
to dwell among the kingdom of words flowering within.

He looked into me and I was his student again,
not understanding a thing, but awakened to a web spun
in which I found myself spinning my own,
to counter the first—the world and its pain.
I hugged him gently, my strength
enough to snap stick bones,
and felt his embrace hanging in the air
long after it dropped away.

Brother in the Dark

He phones out of the blue,
the unfamiliar voice familial.
It's 1976. He's twenty-five,
a grad student already published.
For weeks I've been reading his poems,
wanting at nineteen to be a poet
without knowing what that means.
An hour passes with talk of things
sunk in a memory I can't unlock,
a darkness of time or mind
that nothing can change.
But I remember this part:
he says he read my poems.
I flash to a mutual friend who
must have shown him my crap.
"They're not that bad," he laughs,
his voice like a hand that pulls you
out of a ditch you were digging for hours,
the fading light offset by the laughter
at how little you have dug and
how much deeper you must go.
At some point he says he's returning
to Fresno. We're in Iowa now,
landlocked by rolling cornfields.
I imagine orchards, redwoods, deserts,
and as we're talking a light
beams from that distant coast,
full of presence and silence,
more enduring than memory,
yet living inside it, hidden, until
piercing the dark with a warm voice.
In five years I'll be in California,
a grad student first, then a worker,
at the start of a journey nowhere

and everywhere for sunken moments
and the glimmers of possible futures,
my steps leading into and out of words,
never really knowing anything firm,
but feeling the voice I hear today
running through my days and nights,
in the air, in the blue distance,
in the things that knock us down
and lock us up moment to moment.
That voice is *understanding*,
moving into place when things
come loose. I won't hear it again,
except in poems that outlive him,
poems dreaming words and seeking
to enter lives as night sifts into streets.
I'll feel the lives and deaths he praised,
caught in the moments and breaths
that can't live without words,
and somewhere in them, moving,
restlessly searching, the young poet,
before the earth folded over him,
who offered me his hand.

for Ernesto Trejo (1950-1990)

New Home

Alive again in my dream last night—
white Egyptian cotton dress,
hair all plump with curls,
lips bright as glistening red wax—
my mother stepped forth
and led me through a seam in the air.

We entered a suite of rooms
with mahogany table and chairs,
Persian rug, crystal goblets,
lacy curtains swollen with light.
She said she was happy there,
though her mouth never moved.

What about Pop? I asked,
thinking of the empty house
and our hollow time in the dark.
I didn't feel the grief of death,
only sorrow for unvoiced words
saying how much I loved.

I toured her luxurious home,
all of it as real and solid as life.
She kept to one side, but her joy
reached out like pools of water-light
till the whole place bound me close—
and I awoke at the threshold of words.

The Moth

The moth has died on the threshold
from age or ceaseless flight or perhaps
too much darkness. It couldn't reach
this lamplit house where I face
the blank night dreaming of nations
driven under sod, of words as old
as stones, as mute as peopleless earth.
Now clouds of moths are snowing inside,
their wings fan my eyes, casting shadows
irresistible to death who overthrows
nothing too small. I too
must cross the threshold, leave night
in its cave, and gleam, my body
fed with flame, my words writ in gold.

An Open Letter to John Keats in Æternum

O Keats, pity the heart's holy affections,
its journey along a razor's edge.

Pity its fright at following love's lead across
every border, surrendering too as in an undertow

till drowned in happy darkness.
Tonight I accept what in pain you wrote:

*I have been astonished that men could die
martyrs for religion. I have shudder'd at it.*

*I shudder no more. I could be martyr'd
for my religion. Love is my religion.*

I could die for that. I could die for love.
Your religion of love is much like death,

a fall into shadows and shinings, grace
of blackest light, deepest luminescence.

Inside your becalmed, dreamy gaze
there is desire as fierce as burning gold.

Do you remember from the grave,
can you still remember how it feels

to love and to suffer, how the heart
holds all creation when it is full?

From underground, do you remember
the temple and the warm love?

The casement is set high in the wall,
and a dove trembles into the night.

The wind lifts the gauzy curtains
that slide across two lovers abed—

their ageless heat a penetralium
in which they merge and submerge.

Into this prodigious room, cloaked
from the impending storm without,

you entered with your vivid mirror,
forever calling us. If we choose ardor,

we'll go to that place where you are,
not lost in love and poetry but found;

we'll come at last warmed by starlight
and torches that burn through endless night;

we'll follow you down there, unfleshed, flowing,
and dream ourselves real again.

The Nets by Caspar David Friedrich

There's no meaning in the coarse nets
    spread on misshapen staves to dry;
but the painter stood rapt in their presence,
    watching clouds take up half the sky.
Spellbound birds with wings outstretched
    are reaching, unreaching a hidden moon;
the world in sumptuous night is drenched,
    as waves glisten and puddles swoon.
The eye receives but the heart pours forth,
    and music wells silent in the mind;
stars and wishes fall bloodless to earth,
    caught by arms woven strong and blind.
Past storm and foam and fear they hold,
    sentries by night, fishers in the dawn's gold.

Nacimiento

I was born late in the year,
at the hour when the stars
are bejeweled fish angling
across the sky. I was born
first-son on a Saturday,
seventh day, Saturn's day,
day of faiths. Distant
blue orb ringed in crystals
was my origin. I arrived
into chilly life with frost
flowers tangled in my hair.

Did my mother say my name
or cradle me against her breasts—
her radiance a cloud
hovering above, her breathing
a kind of song? Did my father
grab a quick beer on his way
home from the hospital, shaping
words to fit the becalmed bounty
at year's end? Or dizzy with
lack of sleep and the newness
of being a father, did he slowly
drive across nighttime silence,
drinking in the lights and future?

I'd like to know, for through
such small things run meanings
that catch up to this me writing the page,
if only they can be imagined
more surely than the truth.

On Monitor Street
an apartment waited,
uncrowned heads
coming into focus
and rough hands
swaddling me in words
that guttered the calentón's
honeycombed flames.

Now my fall into life
opens and ends the night.
Like a voice it moves inside
this house, emanating from
candlelight and whiskey shot,
urging me out to the threshold
of my porch, the step into
lustrous space, stars swelling
and falling near through clouds,
a net of trees, midnight bells.

Looking Up and After

I see it on my morning run,
a plain plastic grocery bag
rising, sinking, drifting
through the atmosphere,
the two loops for handgrips
dangling leggish and aslant
while the body, a limpid
airborne sac, balloons.

As a kid I dreamt of flying
over rooftops, dangerous trees,
my webbed outstretched arms
soaring me faster, farther,
closer to the humming sun.
If I wanted to go higher
I simply wished it, and my body
became shadowless, aloft
in the dome of the world.

Sometimes I flew underwater,
schools of angelfish gusting from me,
the sun, a swaying disk of maize,
silent in the firmament's flood.
Deeper down, colder dark lines appeared—
the shadows of baleen or Great Whites,
haunted shipwrecks, the lost Atlantis
whispering in my ears as if
the sea were a dreaming god itself.

Years later I felt that flight in love,
a haven most wanted and reached—
the same place I arrived at
on homemade wings of words.
Every day and night I cast my nets
to hold the sun or catch the sea,
waiting for a sudden leap into
all possibility and the rest of the world.

Today I jog past the city skyline,
past the endless freeway traffic,
running from life's feebleness, from me.
Then I see it up there, prairie bound,
soaring high above the world whose
torment and sweetness no one escapes.
My airy jellyfish skims the pulsing traffic,
all that speed and rage and panic,
and bears me to a place I almost lost.
I'll fly there again tomorrow.

Night of Shooting Stars

Now have you ever heard
how stars fall from the night sky
whenever we wake to the future?
Not the isolated future
with its mishap, its lovely damage,
but the whole of heart's terrain
that floods the deeps of space,
freeing fire from its tedious cage.

Lying on our backs side by side,
earth's mantle drifting below us,
heaven's wheeling race above,
let's count the fiery grains of ice and ash
that skid down the black of time,
and dream another us awaking to light.

Glossary and Notes

escondido: Hidden.

la tierra bonita: The beautiful land.

puto, joto, maricón: Derogatory terms for homosexuals.

velorio: A wake or funeral.

madrina: Godmother.

para los niños: For the children.

caracara: A bird of prey of the falcon family that feeds on carrion.

bajada: The slope of a mountain.

Cipango: The old Chinese name for Japan, first recorded by Marco Polo.

Malinche: Both a name and a derogatory term in Mexican Spanish meaning "traitor" or "sell-out." This animus derives from the fall of Tenochtitlán and conquest of Mexico by the Spanish. Despite the confusing yet fascinating etymology of the word, "Malinche" also signifies tragedy and death.

Anáhuac: Ancient Mexico, literally "land by the waters" (Nahuatl).

Mictlán: One of the underworlds in Aztec mythology, literally "that which is below us" (Nahuatl).

pelados: Penniless oafs, poor slobs, slum dwellers, the underclass or underprivileged generally (literally "bald," "peeled," or "barren")

pan dulce: Mexican pastry in a variety of forms.

pulque: An alcoholic drink made from the agave plant, milky white in appearance with a sour taste. Generally considered a poor man's drink before beer became popular in Mexico.

Tenochtitlán: The ancient name of Mexico City. Linguists are unsure of the etymology of this Nahuatl word, but many believe it means "place of the nopal rock." The cactus was sacred to the sun god.

ya 'cabaron todo: They ruined (literally "ended" or "finished") everything.

abrazo: A hug.

en æternum: In eternity or forever (Latin).

nacimiento: Birth or birthday.

calentón: A small gas space heater.

Pages 4-5 "Cicadas": Male cicadas produce the loud vibrating sound heard during summer. Some species are thought to create a "song." Scholars tell us of the ancient Greeks' admiration for the cicada, whose voice they described as "dewy." In *The Iliad* Homer likens old men to cicadas.

Pages 6-7 "Milton's Taproom": An iconic jazz club/tavern in Kansas City from the 1940s until the 1980s.

Page 13-15 "Velorio": Many Latino wakes have a recitation of the rosary, a form of devotion using a string of beads representing prayers. The rosary at a wake is usually led by a priest. The quoted phrase is from the prayer honoring the mother of God known as "Hail Mary" recited as part of the rosary.

Page 40: "Under the Mountain": Tláloc is the name of the Aztec god of rain, water, lightning, and agriculture. He is associated with mountains and considered the ruler of Tlalocán, the underworld paradise of the Aztecs.

Page 41-42 "After the Discovery": This account of Columbus's voyage to Jamaica is based on Sir Hans Sloane's "A Voyage to the Islands Madera, Barbadoes, Nieves, St. Christophers, and Jamaica, 1707-1725." A few first editions still exist in rare book libraries.

Page 43-44 "Malinche on Cortés": Malinche refers to the name of the Indian guide who led Spanish conqueror Hernán Cortés to the Aztec capitol of Mexico. Her original Nahuatl name was Malinalli. The Spaniards called her "Marina." Historians speculate that the Aztecs thought of Cortés as "Malinche," and since they communicated with him through Malinalli, they also called her "Malinche."

Page 46-48 "A Demon Meets Papa Cayo on the Road to Mictlán": The polytheism of the Aztecs survived Spanish conquest for centuries in Mexico, including the transposition of demons to a Christian context. In popular folklore, Satan and his angels assumed the role of the so-called pagan demons. However, indigenous beliefs persisted, popularized by the writings of Carlos Castañeda, whose *brujos* or sorcerers (aka *naguales*) transform into animals.

Page 49-52 "Banners": El Monte, California, was one of the sites of widespread labor conflict in the 1930s. The movie *Salt of the Earth* depicts how many women participated in strikes, pickets, and organizing. Though unsuccessful, these early labor struggles helped sow the seeds of the Chicano movement in the 1960s.

Page 53-56 "Chronicle of a Salvadoran Girl": This is a version of a poem by the Salvadoran poet José Roberto Cea. The original, "Crónica de una muchacha salvadoreña," comes from his 1968 collection *Todo el Códice*.

Page 64–65 "Brother in the Dark": This poem is about poet Ernesto Trejo. Born in Zacatecas, Mexico, Trejo studied poetry at Fresno State University and the University of Iowa. He wrote beautifully arresting poems in both Spanish and English. As Edward Hirsch has written, Trejo created "magical interior spaces of childhood and [a] luminous floating world" that continue to amaze. He died prematurely of cancer at the age of 40.

Page 67-68 "An Open Letter to John Keats in Æternum": The English Romantic poet Keats became famous for his letters as much as for his poems. Here the italicized passage is from a letter to his fiancée Fanny Brawne, dated October 13, 1819, before tuberculosis ended Keats's life and dream of love. Although his life was brief, the poesis and soulmaking of Keats's life and words endure as a basis for our own experience in time.

Page 69 "The Nets": Caspar David Friedrich (1774-1840) is a German Romantic landscape artist. His paintings offer not only beauty but also moments of the sublime. *Die Netze* (ca. 1830–35) hangs in the Hermitage Museum, Saint Petersburg, Russia.

About the Author

Andrés Rodríguez was born in 1955 in Kansas City. He studied English at the University of Iowa, Stanford, and the University of California. The author of a previous collection of poetry, *Night Song* (Tia Chucha Press), and a work of literary criticism, *Book of the Heart: The Poetics, Letters, and Life of John Keats* (Lindisfarne Press), Rodriguez has published poems in *Blue Mesa Review, Bilingual Review, Cortland Review, Harvard Review, Hubbub, Palabra, Valparaiso Poetry Review*, and other journals. He has also been included in the anthologies *Currents from the Dancing River* (Harcourt Brace), *Dream of a Word* (Tia Chucha Press), *New Chicano/Chicana Writing* (University of Arizona Press), and *Wild Song* (University of Georgia Press). In 2007 he won the Maureen Egan Writers Exchange Award in Poetry sponsored by *Poets & Writers*. He lives and works in Kansas City.

About this Book

This book was typeset by Greg Field in Goudy Old Style, 10 point, and printed on high quality creme paper. It is printed and bound by CreateSpace.

www.ingramcontent.com/pod-product-compliance
Lightning Source LLC
Chambersburg PA
CBHW051734040426
42447CB00008B/1133